A FINE FRENZY
ONE CELL IN THE SEA

T0052885

Alfred Publishing Co., Inc.
16320 Roscoe Blvd., Suite 100
P.O. Box 10003
Van Nuys, CA 91410-0003
alfred.com

ISBN-10: 1-7390-5024-9
ISBN-13: 978-0-7390-5024-8

CONTENTS

COME ON, COME OUT

Words and Music by
ALISON SUDOL, LUKAS BURTON
and HAL CRAGIN

8

C   Cmaj7   Fmaj9

Stay-ing in-side, it all____ goes, all____ goes by._____

C   G   F

3. A

Verse 3:

C   F

blan-ket un - folds,   a blan-ket to lie._____ The

C   F

piec - es of____ gold,_____ they light up your eyes. And

THE MINNOW & THE TROUT

Words and Music by
ALISON SUDOL

14

Bridge:

WHISPER

Words and Music by
ALISON SUDOL and LUKAS BURTON

RANGERS

Words and Music by
ALISON SUDOL, LUKAS BURTON
and HAL CRAGIN

Bridge:

YOU PICKED ME

Words and Music by
ALISON SUDOL, LUKAS BURTON
and HAL CRAGIN

THINK OF YOU

Moderately fast ($\quarternote = 126$)

Words and Music by
ALISON SUDOL

(with pedal)

1. It's

Verse 1:

one hun-dred and nine de-grees__ in this crowd-ed room,__ no

room to breathe,__ with walls as cold__ as a gal-ler-y.__

Verse 2:

thought I had__ it fig-ured out__ in a brand-new life__ with a great big house_ and

green_ i - ni - tials on the tow'ls. I should be hap-py now.__ Well, you've

got your-self__ a fam-i - ly__ and you plant-ed roots_ down by the sea.__ I

D.S. % al Coda

saw you once__ on the street,__ you did-n't no - tice me.__ But I

Chorus:

think of you when-ev-er life gets me down. I

think of you when-ev-er you're not a-round.

And you rest your bones

some-where far from my own,

ALMOST LOVER

Words and Music by
ALISON SUDOL

Slowly (♩ = 63)

1. Your fin - ger -

Verse 1:

tips a - cross my skin, the palm trees sway - ing in the wind;___ im - ag - es.___

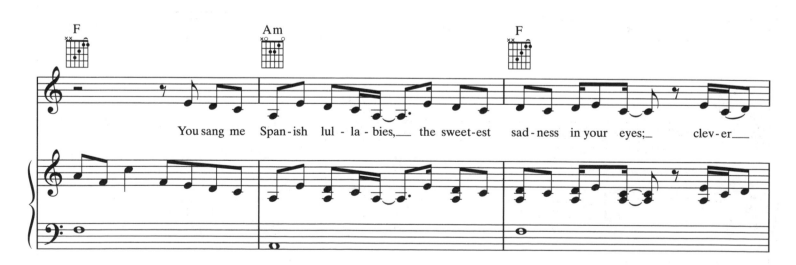

You sang me Span - ish lul - la - bies,___ the sweet - est sad - ness in your eyes;___ clev - er___

Almost Lover - 6 - 1
29110

ASHES AND WINE

Gtr. tuned down 1/2 step:
⑥ = E♭ ③ = G♭
⑤ = A♭ ② = B♭
④ = D♭ ① = E♭

Words and Music by
ALISON SUDOL, LUKAS BURTON
and HAL CRAGIN

Chorus:

to say._____ But

is there____ a chance,____ a frag - ment of light_____ at the end____ of the tun -

nel, a rea - son to fight?_____ Is there____ a chance____ you may____ change your mind,___

or are we ash - es and wine,_____

dim.

mf

re - duced to ash - es_____ and wine,_____

or are we ash - es?

Verse 2:
Don't know if our fate's already sealed.
This day's a spinning circus on a wheel.
And I'm ill with the thought of your kiss,
Coffee-laced, intoxicating on her lips.
Shut it out, I've got no claim on you now.
I'm not allowed to wear your freedom down, no.
(To Chorus:)

NEAR TO YOU

Words and Music by
ALISON SUDOL and NICKLAS SAMPLE

1. He and I had some-thing beau-ti-ful, but so dys-
(2.) you and I have some-thing dif-fer-ent, and I'm en-

func-tion-al, it could-n't last. I
joy-ing it cau-tious-ly. I'm

Bridge:

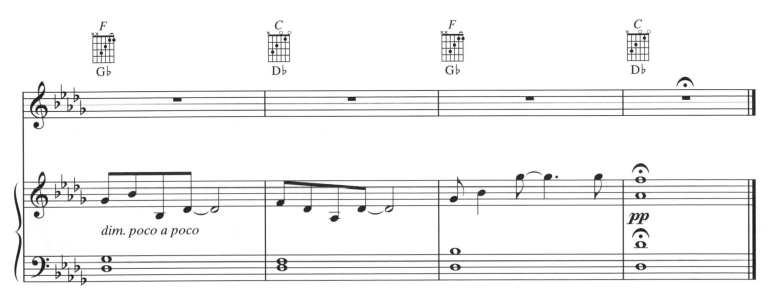

LIAR, LIAR

Words and Music by
ALISON SUDOL

Gtr. tuned down 1/2 step:

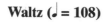

Waltz (♩ = 108)

N.C.

(Accordion)

Moderate rock (♩ = 120)

Guitar → E

Piano → E♭

A/C♯

A♭/C

A

A♭

E

E♭

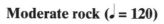

Liar, Liar - 8 - 1
29110

Verse:

1. Li - ar, li - ar, you're such a great big li - ar,
2. Sick and tir - ed of this mad de - si - re,

with the tall - est tales that I have ev - er heard.
flut - ter - ing in - side me like a hawk.

Fi - re, fi - re, you set my soul on
Wi - re, wi - re, you've got my hands on

fi - re, laugh - ing in the cor -
wi - res. Well, heav - en help you when

Chorus:

Bridge:

All the ships go down

fol - low - ing the sound.

All the ships go down.

LAST OF DAYS

Words and Music by
ALISON SUDOL

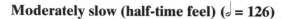

Moderately slow (half-time feel) (♩ = 126)

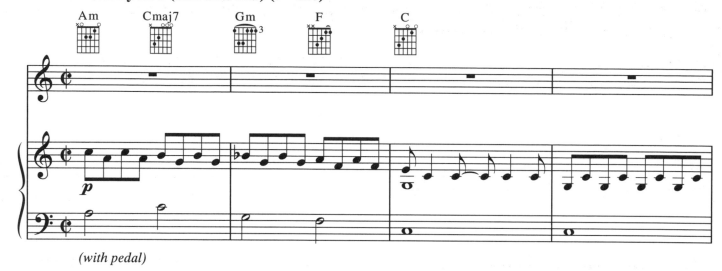

(with pedal)

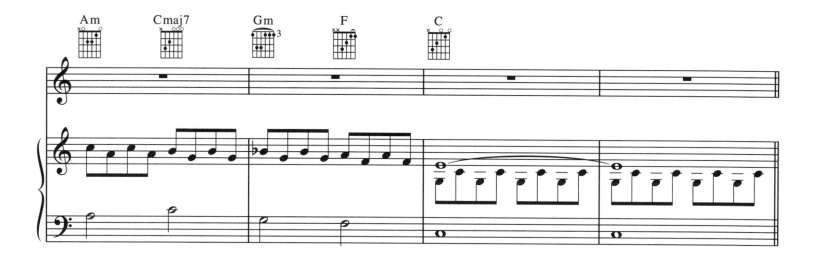

Verse:

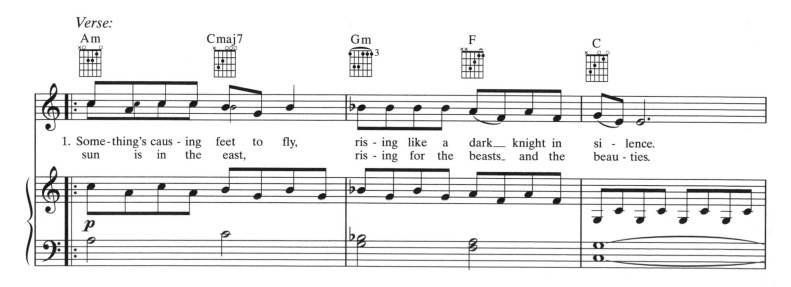

1. Some-thing's caus-ing feet to fly, ris-ing like a dark__ knight in the si - lence.

sun is in the east, ris-ing for the beasts__ and the beau - ties.

70 *Bridge:*

wars_____ and har - vest moons,_____

I_____ will wait_____ for you._____

D.S. % al Coda

The

dim.

til the___ last of days,___

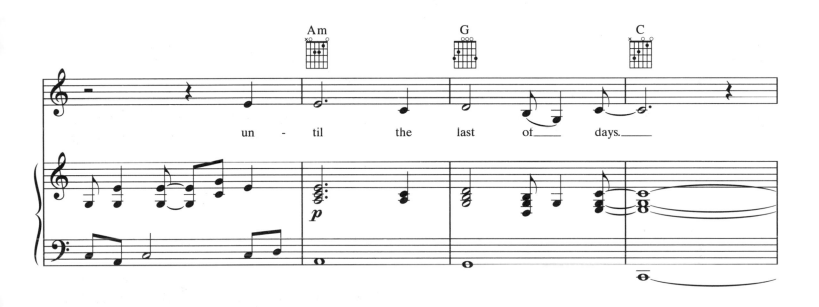

un - til the last of___ days.___

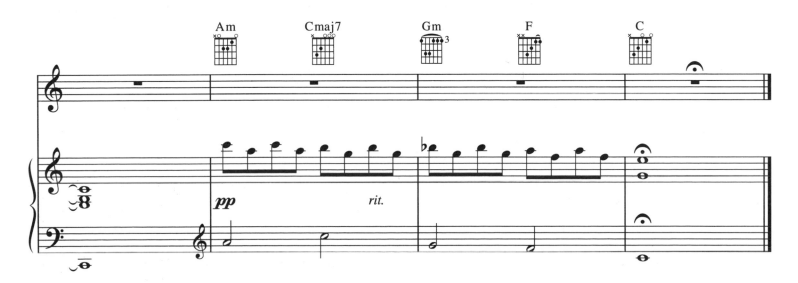

LIFESIZE

Words and Music by
ALISON SUDOL, LUKAS BURTON
and HAL CRAGIN

Lifesize - 8 - 1
29110

Verse 1:

1. We stood___ so tall,___ we caught___ a plane___ by___ the wing___ and held___ it safe___ un-til___ we found___ it a place___ to___ land. We laid___ a-cross___ the o - cean wide,___ bridged___ the gap___ in rec - ord time.___

(1st time only; lead vocal ad lib. through repeats)

Great in the eyes_____ of some - one._____

HOPE FOR THE HOPELESS

Words and Music by
ALISON SUDOL, LUKAS BURTON
and HAL CRAGIN

Verse 2:

Chorus:

There's   hope.

BORROWED TIME

Words and Music by
ALISON SUDOL and ANTHONY PENALOZA

Bridge:

Chorus:

Step, step right o - ver the line and on - to bor - rowed time. When it's life, not wait - ing to die, wait - ing to di - vide, to di - vide.